◆ In Celebration of ◆

A special book
for your
special day!

Ort & Datum

Name

Wishes

Picture of the day

Name

Wishes

Picture of the day

Name

Wishes

Picture of the day

Name

Wishes

Picture of the day

_____

Name

Wishes

_____

_____

_____

_____

_____

_____

_____

Picture of the day

Name

Wishes

Picture of the day

_____

Name

Wishes

_____

_____

_____

_____

_____

_____

_____

Picture of the day

Name

Wishes

Picture of the day

Name

Wishes

Picture of the day

Name

Wishes

Picture of the day

Name

Wishes

Picture of the day

Name

Wishes

Picture of the day

Name

Wishes

Picture of the day

Name

Wishes

Picture of the day

Name

Wishes

Picture of the day

Name

Wishes

Picture of the day

Name

Wishes

Picture of the day

Name

Wishes

Picture of the day

Name

Wishes

Picture of the day

Name

Wishes

Picture of the day

Name

Wishes

Picture of the day

Name

Wishes

Picture of the day

Name

Wishes

Picture of the day

Name

Wishes

Picture of the day

Name

Wishes

Picture of the day

Name

Wishes

Picture of the day

Name

Wishes

Picture of the day

Name

Wishes

Picture of the day

Name

Wishes

Picture of the day

_____
Name

Wishes

_____

_____

_____

_____

_____

_____

_____

Picture of the day

Name

Wishes

Picture of the day

Name

Wishes

Picture of the day

Name

Wishes

Picture of the day

Name

Wishes

Picture of the day

_____

Name

Wishes

_____

_____

_____

_____

_____

_____

_____

Picture of the day

Name

Wishes

Picture of the day

Name

Wishes

Picture of the day

_____

Name

Wishes

_____

_____

_____

_____

_____

_____

_____

Picture of the day

Name

Wishes

Picture of the day

Name

Wishes

Picture of the day

Name

Wishes

Picture of the day

Name

Wishes

Picture of the day

Name

Wishes

Picture of the day

_____
Name

Wishes

_____

_____

_____

_____

_____

_____

_____

Picture of the day

Name

Wishes

Picture of the day

Name

Wishes

Picture of the day

Name

Wishes

Picture of the day

Name

Wishes

Picture of the day

_____

Name

Wishes

_____

_____

_____

_____

_____

_____

_____

Picture of the day

Name

Wishes

Picture of the day

Name

Wishes

Picture of the day

Name

Wishes

Picture of the day

_____

Name

Wishes

_____

_____

_____

_____

_____

_____

_____

Picture of the day

_____

Name

Wishes

_____

_____

_____

_____

_____

_____

_____

Picture of the day

Name

Wishes

Picture of the day

Name

Wishes

Picture of the day

Name

Wishes

Picture of the day

_____

Name

Wishes

_____

_____

_____

_____

_____

_____

_____

Picture of the day

Name

Wishes

Picture of the day

Made in the USA
Middletown, DE
01 March 2023

25992563R00071